65

HOW THE FUCK DID THAT HAPPEN

MW01096900

Copyright © 2022

All rights reserved. No part of this publication may be reproduced, distributed, or transmitted in any form or by any means, including photocopying, recording, or other electronic or mechanical methods, without the prior or written permission of the publisher

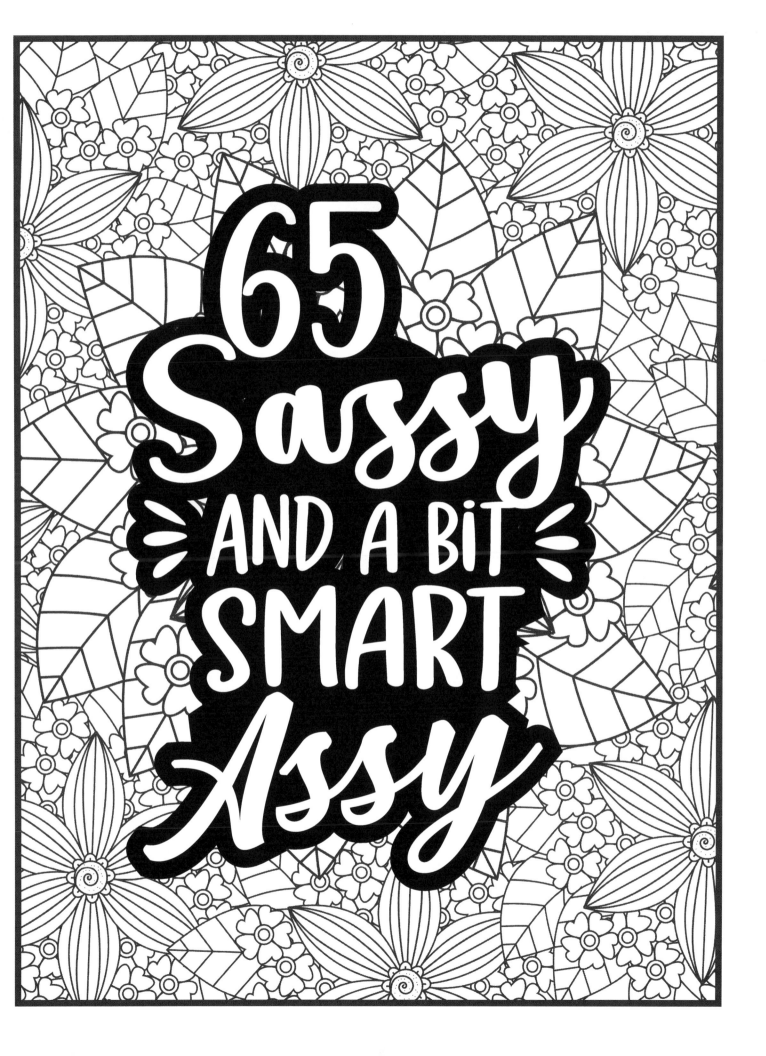

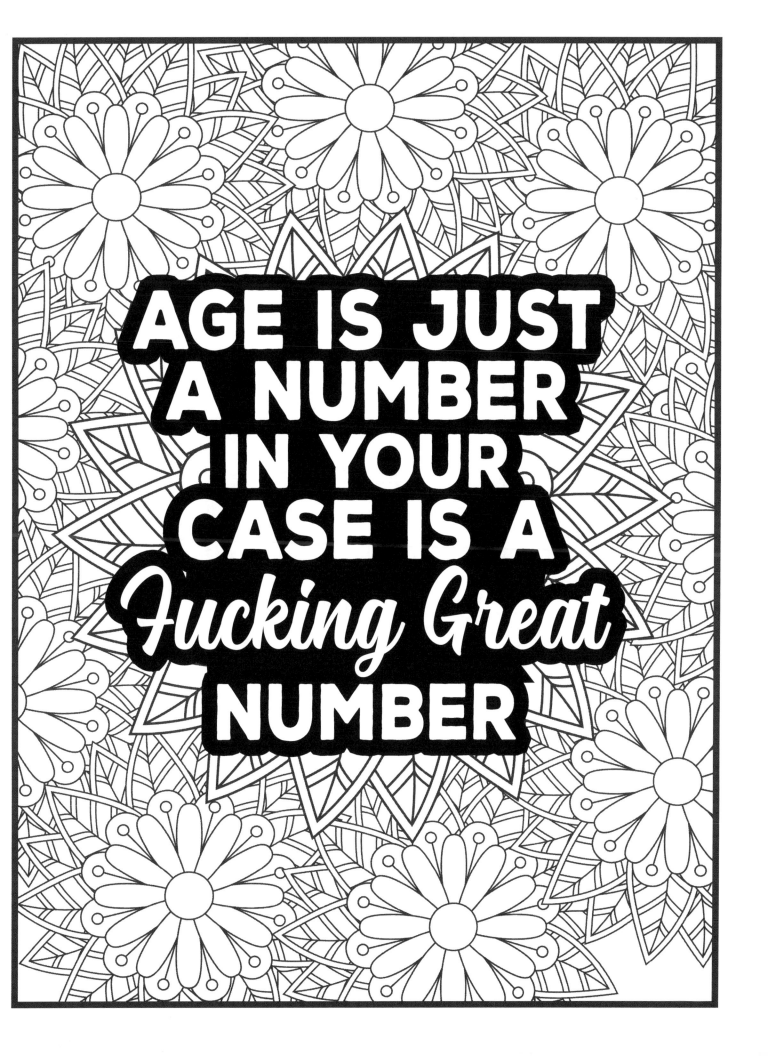

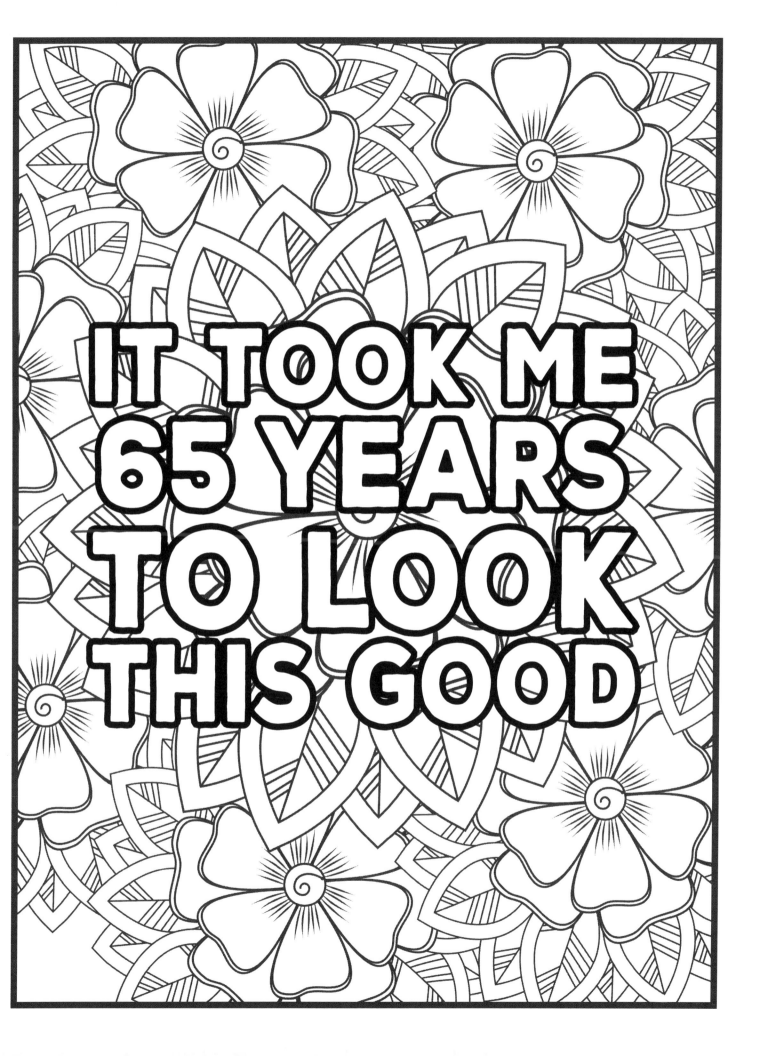

Test Your Colors

☆ ☆ ☆ ☆ ☆
Don't forget to
give us your opinion
By leaving a review

Made in United States
Troutdale, OR
03/17/2024

18542846R00046